MEDITATIONS

with

JAMES VAN PRAAGH

A FIRESIDE BOOK
PUBLISHED BY SIMON & SCHUSTER

NEW YORK   LONDON   TORONTO   SYDNEY

FIRESIDE
Rockefeller Center
1230 Avenue of the Americas
New York, NY 10020

FIRESIDE and colophon are registered trademarks
of Simon & Schuster, Inc.

For information regarding special discounts for bulk purchases,
please contact Simon & Schuster Special Sales at 1-800-456-6798
or business@simonandschuster.com.

DESIGNED BY RUTH LEE-MUI

Manufactured in the United States of America

10 8 6 4 2   3 5 7 9

Library of Congress Cataloging-in-Publication Data

Van Praagh, James.
Meditations/with James van Praagh.
p.cm.
1. Spiritualism. 2. Meditations. I. Title.
BF1261.2.V355 2003
158.1'2—dc22
2003059190

ISBN 0-7432-2943-6

✤ Contents ✤

MEDITATION
PRELIMINARIES

You are about to explore a new world, a new universe all its own—the world of your inner being. This world is available to anyone who will take the time to become aware. By opening to your inner self, you bring a new consciousness into every aspect of your life. You begin to live a more fulfilled existence and a happier life.

❧ The Importance of Meditation ❧

Nowadays it seems that the world is spinning out of control with one tragedy after another, and our safety and security can no longer be taken for granted. Yet amid this outer turmoil, there is a place where we can find peace and understanding and a world of unlimited potential and promise. This safe haven of beauty and love lies inside ourselves. You and I are multidimensional beings residing in a divine universe. This is our true reality and our spiritual birthright. When we turn off the outer physical world and tune in to the silence of this inner beauty, we will find the peace that surpasses all understanding.

The easiest and most dependable way to tune inside is through meditation. Meditation is a process whereby we balance our emotional, mental, physical, and spiritual selves in the silence of our natural state of being. It is here that we will find the safety and security we seek. When we meditate or concentrate our energies on the spiritual nature within us, we will learn to recognize the oneness and wholeness of all of life.

Meditation is a way to move into a consciousness of real *knowing*. As we sit silently and focus our attention inwardly, we start to become aware of our true self. The more we meditate, the stronger this awareness becomes, and the more we are able to let go of our stress and deal with life's situations with ease and certainty. Our doubts, insecurities, and anxieties diminish in size because we no longer feel separated from our good. If you meditate every day, you will definitely feel better about your life.

When you meditate, you activate cosmic energies. These forces illuminate and energize the spiritual centers inside the body. The light of unconditional love is lit within you and continues to grow with each meditation. The more you transform yourself through this light of unconditional love, the more you can influence others in a positive way.

*W*hen you begin your inner work, you need first to make a clear dedication to yourself. You must be motivated to work on yourself, but without a particular goal. Any time you pursue a meditative practice, you are making a commitment to understand yourself more fully as a spiritual being. This takes time, even lifetimes. Be patient with your practice.

❧ The Ways to Meditate ❧

There is no one way to meditate. When people hear the word "meditation," they think of sitting cross-legged on the floor, incense burning, candles lit, and someone chanting "Om." This is one way of meditating. However, meditation has many forms. Prayer is a form of meditation. When you pray, you focus on God. You surrender your burdens to the divine and ask for assistance in your life situations. When you meditate, you surrender your outer world to be in your inner world. Meditation is not about brooding over problems and running them over in your head. That is neither prayer nor meditation; it is simply spinning your wheels.

Another way you can meditate is by tapping in to your creative energies, such as by writing, painting, and music. There are a variety of meditative processes whereby you focus your mind inwardly. Go with whatever works for you.

The processes that I recommend in this book are contemplative and prayerlike. The best way that I have found to meditate is to sit in an upright position in a chair. Sitting up straight allows the energies to flow more easily up and down the spiritual centers of the body. Keep your feet flat on the floor with your palms open and facing up on your thighs. If you sit on the floor, you can use the cross-legged yoga position. Wear loose, comfortable clothing so that you won't be distracted by anything tight or binding on your body.

Meditation is not a nap, although you may feel as if you had one. Usually after quieting your mind for any period of time, you do feel recharged. Think of meditation as focused concentration for a specific purpose. The purpose is to know the real you.

If your time is limited, or if you are new to meditation, start with five minutes a day. Remember that it doesn't matter if you are commuting to work on a train or bus, or sitting at your desk, or on a park bench at lunchtime: You can meditate anywhere. The time spent in the silence of your divine self is probably the most important time you will ever spend.

The practice of meditation is designed to increase self-awareness. It becomes a way of life and will assist you especially when you fall back into patterns of negative thinking and self-torment.

A Sacred Space

I am fortunate to have a meditation room in my home. It's a room that I have set aside for my spiritual work. The area has a feeling of respect and reverence. A corner in your bedroom can serve as that special place of silence to commune with your spiritual self. You may want to set a table nearby and place holy pictures, prayer beads, and flowers on it. Many people erect altars in their homes for their religious practices. You can make your space into whatever suits you. Adding candles, crystals, and incense will help to heighten the senses.

Use this sacred space as your spiritual work area only. It is important that it is clear of clutter. Begin each meditation in an atmosphere where you will not be bothered by outside distractions. Turn off the phones, beepers, fax machines, and answering machines. Turn off anything that could interrupt your concentration and interfere with your inner journey. You can play soft music to help set a mood for inner focus. Creating an atmosphere that is peaceful will help you to be receptive to the higher vibrations of spirit.

When you meditate, you want to turn off the outside world so that the beauty and splendor of the spiritual dimensions of the soul can be revealed.

Spacing Out

People often ask me if being "spaced out" is the same as being in a meditative state. Not necessarily. I always recommend that you stay awake and aware. Your eyes may be closed, but you are still aware of your surroundings. When you space out, you leave your body open to any and all energy vibrations of consciousness. If you have not created a strong inner spiritual core, lower energies can be attracted to you. These vibrations may cause you to feel irritable and unbalanced. Being a "space cadet" doesn't necessarily mean being in tune with the God force energy within. In fact, spacing out can be dangerous. I always urge people to be grounded and stable, totally aware of their physical space. When you remain present and in control of your body during meditation, you can accomplish much more of what you want.

You must give yourself time to meditate. It doesn't matter what time of the day you do it—morning, noon, or night. A few minutes of uninterrupted peace every day will produce healing results.

The Basics ∾

Before you do any of the meditations, I suggest you practice the following basic exercises for several days until you are thoroughly acquainted with them. These basic preparations are aimed at quieting your mind and emotions in order to center your awareness within. If possible, close your eyes for all the meditation exercises so that distractions are minimized.

When doing any of the meditations in the book, you may want to read them over several times before visualizing what you have just read. Doing this may take time at first, but if you commit to daily meditation practice, you will find that going within becomes natural and effortless.

Remember that when you meditate, you are in the process of releasing various thoughts, feelings, and physical discomforts. As you let them go, the God force energy within you begins to free you from the burdens you have been carrying. There is no more struggle to control things. You realize that everything in life moves in its own rhythm and its own time. One example is your own breathing.

There is an invisible, infinite part of ourselves that I call the soul. The soul is our spiritual core; it is the divine spark of life that always was and forever will be. Think of this spark as a light that burns brightly within you. This is the essence of who you are, and it is contained in each breath you take.

Breath of Life

As you breathe, think of life moving in and out of your body. Your breath refreshes and recharges your space and all your energy systems. Whenever you feel anxious, fearful, or confused, take a deep breath, and let your breath tap into the depth of your knowingness.

Start by closing your eyes and concentrating on your breathing. Focus as your breath goes in and out. Make sure that you are taking slow, deep breaths from your midsection, not shallow, quick breaths from your throat area. Breathe in fresh, clean air and hold it for a count of four, then breathe out through your mouth to a count of four. As you do, imagine all the tension and strains of the day leaving your body as a gray mist.

When thoughts pop up in your mind, let them go as you continue to concentrate on your breathing.

After five or six deep inhalations and exhalations, just let your breath follow its own natural rhythm. You will soon become aware of the rise and fall of your breath much like the ebb and flow of the ocean tide. After a while, your mind will become more still. You will feel more calm and in harmony with your own self. Your mind will be open to a deep, spiritual awareness.

When your body is relaxed, you have let go of all the stress you have been holding in every muscle, organ, and fiber of your being. You give your body time to renew and regenerate tissue. Relaxation helps your body tap into the spiritual vitality that sustains it.

✎ Relaxation Technique ✎

Relaxation is the key to any meditation. It's hard to focus on anything, especially your inner self, when you feel tense or emotionally unbalanced. This exercise will help you release stress and get more comfortable.

Begin with your breathing technique. After you are centered in the rhythm of your breath, envision each part of your body, one at a time, starting with your toes. Tighten your toes and then relax them. Move your awareness up to your legs, tighten them, and relax. Tighten your thighs front and back, and let go. Then move up to your hips and buttocks; tighten these muscles, and relax them. You will begin to feel the soreness and stress in your body leaving. Your pelvic area is next. Again tighten the muscles, then let go. Keep breathing. Move up to the stomach. Tighten the muscles with your breath, and then release the tension. Next, do the same with your chest and back. By now you will begin to feel even more relaxed. Next, tighten the muscles in your neck. This is an area where we store a lot of tension. Relax your neck and squeeze your shoulders together, and then relax them. Let out a sigh if you wish. Move your attention to your arms. Tighten your biceps and let go. Make a fist with each hand, then release all the tension. Finally, squeeze up your face, around your eyes and mouth, and then relax your face. See all the residual tension form into a gray mist and escape out your fingertips and toes. Sit for a few moments and enjoy your relaxed state before you begin your meditation.

*S*piritually minded people usually think for themselves. They are less likely to follow the distorted views of the mass consciousness. When we meditate and envision ourselves as spiritual beings of light and love, we reacquaint ourselves with the true meaning of God.

Grounding

Everything you do involves awareness, and awareness of the energy around you is important while you meditate. Close your eyes and become mindful of the breath. Begin to feel the breath travel deep inside your body. As you relax, let go of the day's concerns. After a few minutes of deep breathing and relaxation, envision a cord gently tied around each ankle. See these cords going into the floor and down to the very center of Earth. When they reach Earth's center, envision two big boulders, and tie each of the cords to a boulder. Next, envision a cord tied from your tailbone going through the floor and down to the center of Earth. Tie this cord to another boulder in Earth's core.

As you visualize the energy of Earth, imagine the color of Earth. It may be reddish brown, green, or whatever color represents Earth to you. See this force of Earth rising from the boulders up the cords and into your ankles and tailbone. Let this energy continue to flow into your body, up your legs and torso and into your heart.

Next, imagine a golden beam of light about two inches above your head. This is the cosmic light of universal energy. Let this light stream down into your head, neck, shoulders, and chest until it reaches your heart. This golden light blends together with Earth's energy and enables you to feel grounded, stabilized, and more centered.

Finally, visualize half the universal energy and half the Earth energy blend together and rise up from your spine and out the top of your head. Let it flow down your body like a fountain of force pouring over you. Just see it flowing over and over until you feel recharged. In this centered and calm state, you are now ready and prepared to begin your meditation exercise.

When you meditate, you enter your own private sanctuary and tap into the purity of higher consciousness where ignorance, judgment, and hostility do not exist.

✎ Inner Sanctuary ✎

Many of the meditations in the book include visualizations, or inner pictures, to help you attain a specific purpose. I suggest that you create a scene in your mind's eye that is conducive to feeling safe and calm. Think of something right now that evokes a feeling of inner security and harmony. It might be a garden. You can envision yourself sitting on a swing or a garden bench under your favorite tree or surrounded by a patch of colorful and fragrant flowers. Design your sanctuary with as much creativity as possible. You are limited only by your imagination. Picture your favorite flowers—roses, lavender, lilies—whichever you prefer. Not only see them but experience their essence as well. Become aware of their appearance, aroma, and distinct individuality.

Perhaps your sanctuary is a park where you see children playing on the swings or hear them off in the distance. You find a spot on the grass under a shady oak or elm tree. There may be a brook nearby, and you can hear the sound of water trickling down the pebbles and stones.

Your sanctuary might be at the seashore or on the banks of a river. Visualize your special place on the sand or on a grassy knoll. As you relax in this sacred area, the water seems so inviting, soothing and tranquil, and you feel completely calm and at peace.

Perhaps you have chosen a meadow or a cabin on a mountaintop as your inner sanctuary. From a vantage point high up, you can see for miles. There may be snowcapped vistas under an unlimited clear blue sky. Experience the world from this remarkable view. Enjoy the scent of clean mountain air that is so invigorating and refreshing.

Whatever your sanctuary setting, make sure that it feels natural and good to you.

MEDITATIONS

*W*hen you are unaware, or live life as an unconscious person, it's as if you are on automatic pilot, paying little attention to how your actions affect your life and other people. One of the most important lessons to learn is to be true to your self. In order to do this, you must be centered in your own self-awareness.

⋙ Centering Yourself ⋘

You are born into this world not empty-handed, but with the wisdom of eternity contained in your soul's memory. It is your job to reconnect with that memory and find your true purpose in life. When you transcend your personality and ego, and center yourself in this eternal wisdom, you clear the way to experience a true union with your divine self.

In the stillness of your relaxed state, imagine a white light far above your head, as if coming from the heavens. As you inhale, see this light coming down to you and surrounding your body. You are bathed in this beautiful light of God. Next envision the light moving through your body. See it enter the top of your head and travel down your throat, chest, into your arms and hands. You are being filled with God's divine light. Continue to see the light move through the rest of your body—your stomach, back, hips, legs, and feet. Every cell in your body is being filled with the white light of God. The light is ever flowing through your body and around your whole energy field. Continue to see the light spilling over you until you *become* the light. This light represents unconditional love, purity, and wholeness. *Be still and know that you are God.* Center yourself in the truth of this knowledge.

*E*verything is energy vibrating at different rates of speed and at different levels of awareness. Your mind, body, and spirit are composed of this same energy, each vibrating at a different frequency. Think of your energy as one unifying force that is connected to everything.

The Energy Around You

Become aware of the space above and below you, as well as in front, behind, and on either side of you. This is your energy field, so become familiar with your own space. Now open your hands so that the palms of your hands are facing each other. Place all your attention on the area between your palms. Sense the feeling between your palms. Move your palms closer together. Feel the warmth of your own energy. Move your hands up and down and feel the energy shifting. You might have to do this a couple of times to really notice the subtle differences.

Hold one hand three inches from any part of your body. How does it feel? Can you tell the subtle energy shifts as you move your hand to another part of your body? Perhaps one part of your body holds a lot of emotional energy. It may feel hot or charged or heavy. Perhaps you can feel the spot where an old injury exists because a concentration of energy is present.

As you continue to feel the energy around your body, sense whether it is heavy or light, hot or cold. Are you able to sense colors around you? Can you see any shapes or faces? Does the energy have a personality of its own? Sit there and become aware of the energy field around you.

If the energy is dense, sluggish, or doesn't feel like your own, this is the time to change it. Imagine a big, bright, golden sun shining above you. Let the heat and light of the sun surround and envelop you. As the sun touches your entire energy field, the atmosphere around and through you begins to clear. Concentrate on the sun filling your space. Is there a noticeable difference? Continue to visualize the sun's rays permeating you until their glow lightens up your entire energy field.

*W*hen I work with people, it is important that my environment is balanced, peaceful, quiet, and pleasant. I can tell immediately if someone is nervous, angry, scared, open, or closed, because I can feel the energy surrounding this person.

A Peaceful and Calm Environment

As you sit in a relaxed state, mindful of the rhythm of your breath, imagine a golden light entering your body and illuminating each organ, muscle, cell, until you are completely filled with light. This golden light is made of joy, balance, calmness, and love, and it brings this sense of peace to all areas of your inner being.

In your mind's eye visualize a lake. Upon its surface are ripples and currents moving in all different directions. These ripples represent your noisy, chaotic thoughts and feelings. As you continue to breathe in the golden light of love, imagine the ripples diminishing and disappearing until there is one tiny ripple.

Notice how still the lake has become. Notice how quiet your mind can be. Continue to breathe in this stillness, and let any last remaining anxieties and uncertainties that are stored in your consciousness exit your breath as a gray mist. As you exhale, let the upset evaporate into this gray mist and watch as it is absorbed into the golden light. Continue to work with your breath until you have replaced your restlessness with stillness. Let your whole being become one of calm and peace.

The truth is, everything you want to know is already inside you. You just have forgotten it. Instead of feeling lost, confused, or lonely, recognize that you are a spiritual being who is part of a large cosmic family of spiritual beings.

❧ Listening to the Silence ❧

The times just after waking and just before sleeping are when our subconscious minds are more receptive to suggestion. The following is a good meditation to do just before going to sleep. Make sure when you sit in bed that your spine is straight against some pillows. Have a pen and pad by your side. Inhale slowly and exhale all the stress. As you inhale, see the oxygen molecules enter your body as healing energy. As you exhale, release all the stagnant energy accumulated during the day.

As you sit in the awareness of the rhythm of your breath, begin to write down any thoughts that enter your mind. If a person comes to mind, write down his or her name. You don't have to write full sentences, just a word or two. Make a list of all the thoughts no matter how silly or stupid they may be. Eventually your mind will begin to quiet down because you have taken the energy of your thoughts and have released it on to the paper. There will be moments when nothing comes to mind. When something pops up, write it down. Enjoy the silence in between your thoughts.

When you have finished, review what you have written. Notice the difference between what you wrote at the beginning of the exercise and what you wrote toward the end, when your mind had cleared itself of clutter. You may have gotten some good ideas with which to follow through.

When we meditate, we are in essence training our thoughts to lift to a higher vibration. Although we may not think anything is going, we are aligning our energy fields to a divine consciousness of love. Many people refer to this consciousness as God. When thoughts are elevated to the God consciousness level, we develop an appreciation of love, joy, calmness, and patience.

Like Attracts Like

Our minds are sources of unlimited potential. They are far more expansive than the capacity of our brains. A universal energy called universal mind links all minds and thoughts together. We tap into this universal mind every time we think. This mind has no boundaries and no limitations. Although they are invisible, thoughts are energy units that go out from us into the universal mind and return to us.

To attain the things you say you want, your thoughts must focus on the positive aspects of life. Begin by focusing on the idea of peace inside you. Inhale and say to yourself *"PEACE,"* and as you exhale, release confusion and chaos. When your mind wanders, bring your awareness back to the word "peace." Let a sense of peace fill your space. Continue this thought of "Peace" until you find that you become calm and more centered.

Imagine that your mind works like a radio station. Its job is to send out and receive signals to everyone and everything on the planet. These thought signals go out like radio waves and connect to a giant transmitting tower called universal mind. These waves bounce off the transmitting tower and are sent out to others. Every thought you think is a signal from your station going out into the universe. At the same time, others are sending messages back to you.

As you meditate, say to yourself: I want to receive only the healthiest and happiest of signals from others. In order to do so, you have to send out thoughts of health, happiness, peace, and contentment. Envision your thoughts as light beams being transmitted from your mental radio station. Let these thoughts go out into the universe as ones of prosperity, approval, harmony, and friendship. These positive thoughts are reaching people in need of love and happiness. As they receive your good thoughts, they begin to smile, and their happy thoughts come back to you. Feel these good thoughts in your heart.

There is a quiet satisfaction deep inside you. Your thoughts and ideas of a higher, spiritual nature are being received by others and are returning to you in kind. You feel alive, refreshed, and transformed in this new awareness.

Thoughts are like magnets—they attract situations and people that reflect what you are thinking. If you are centered in peace and think thoughts that are kind and loving, you will attract the same kind of ideas and feelings back to you. Can you imagine if everyone thought of love and not hatred, of abundance instead of greed? Your thoughts have the power to create good in the world.

Clear Out the Negative

If you have been a negative-thinking person, it may take time to change your thoughts to a higher perspective. Patience and practice are necessary. Just as you have been persisting in the negative thought, you must persist in the positive one.

Focus your attention on the center of your forehead between your eyes. This is your third eye center, the seat of knowing. In this third eye center, imagine a large pink rose. See it open slowly petal by petal. With this beautiful open rose, scan your energy space. Begin at your head. Can you see any images? Do you recognize a face? Do you hear anything? Are your impressions associated with loving, happy thoughts? Or are they ones of fear, sadness, or anxiety? If you experience the latter, place the person, situation, or thought in the middle of the rose, and watch as the rose absorbs the negative energy until it is gone.

Repeat this process in your neck, shoulders, arms, and the rest of your body. Visualize the rose absorbing your negative thoughts. When you have completely scanned your energy space, let the rose float up, up, and away and burst into thousands of tiny specks that dissolve into space.

Then imagine a beautiful green color surrounding your entire space. This represents healing, balance, and harmony. Finally, see a beautiful white rose in your third eye center. This rose represents strength, optimism, and peace of mind. You have cleared the space for your mind to grow and expand with a new awareness.

*W*hen you send out love, a person receives that love. It may not be detected on a conscious level, but it is nevertheless very alive and effective. The more you send out love, the more you receive love back.

The Waterfall of Light

All of us accumulate many beliefs from our parents, teachers, and religions. Some may be good, and some may be outdated or no longer viable. How often have you heard yourself say, "I sound just like my mother (or father)"? Their words are still lodged inside our minds. This exercise will help to empty your head of other people's words and beliefs that no longer have a use in your life.

As you quiet your mind, listen to the thoughts that flow in and out. Become aware of what they are. Do you repeat these words to yourself every day until they have become routine?

Visualize yourself sitting in a shallow stream of

water under a gentle cascading waterfall. The water feels so refreshing as it flows over your whole body. See this waterfall as a shower of liquid light. As the waterfall of light pours over you, it has a very calming effect on your mind. In fact, it washes out the old habitual thoughts, and you find that you have more clarity to think for yourself. All those outdated ideas and beliefs are washed away. You can see them floating down the stream as little soapy bubbles. Watch as they disappear from sight.

As the waterfall of light continues to wash over you, you have a new sense of mindfulness. Your thoughts are now cheerful and constructive. As the liquid light of water continues to flow, do not judge your thoughts. Be ready to experience something wonderful and inspirational. You are opening your mind to the vastness and the greatness of your limitless soul. It is inevitable that your life must begin to change.

The words we heard as children are lodged in our subconscious minds, and these memories are very much alive within us. In order to be in control of your life, you need to reevaluate the ideas and words you heard as a child. Focus on the ones that are hopeful, make you feel confident, and give you a sense of self-worth, and let go of the ones that don't.

ও Affirm Your Good ও

Before you get out of bed in the morning, take a moment to greet your day with a positive tone. Think of something that you would like to say each day that will create the kind of life that you want. For example, "I love myself more each day." "I do only what is good for me." "I bless everyone and every situation that comes my way."

As you go through the day and a negative thought enters your mind, take control of it. Say "Stop!" or "No!" to that thought. Replace it with a positive new thought. If you don't replace the old thought with something new, the old one will persist. For instance, if the thought is: "I don't have money," say: "I have plenty of money to do what I want to do." If the thought is: "I am lonely, I don't have anyone to love me," say: "The world is full of wonderful people. I deserve the perfect person coming into my life."

Don't be discouraged if your rational mind intervenes and reasons that the new thought isn't really true. It's testing you. Are you willing to stick with the new thought even though the situation is not that way now? Be persistent even when you think it is foolish. After all, you've been practicing the negative thought so long, it's become your reality. Practice the new one until it, too, becomes real. It doesn't work if you think "I *can*" once, then the rest of the day you think "I can't, I don't, or I'm never going to."

Do your affirmations in the present tense. Don't say *I will*. Using the future tense means that your good is out there somewhere waiting to come to you. You want to affirm that your good is with you *right now*. Also, it is not enough to think or say the words; you have to *feel* their content, as well. Affirmations are more effective when your thoughts and feelings match.

If you cannot think of any positive affirmations,

use the one I often say to myself: "Happy am I, healthy am I, holy am I." Let these words sink into your mind and heart. By replacing negative words with positive ones, you will begin to feel more self-assured and trusting of life.

Think of today as an opportunity to discover and grow beyond your mental and emotional discomfort. When a difficult situation is upon you, reach into the depth of your being and find a greater meaning to your life and your purpose on Earth. Some of the deepest agonies are the greatest triumphs for your soul's evolution.

❧ Release the Past ❧

Rejection, fear, loneliness, loss, and struggle are some of life's most bitter pills. We would rather deny the pain than feel it. When you live in the past, you cannot resolve your problems and enjoy the moment. You stay stuck in yesterday and struggle to move forward. This exercise will help you to let go of the past and create a space for new opportunities. In hindsight, it's easy to think you could have made a better decision. To me, there are no mistakes. Your soul chooses the unique circumstances and situations in your life as lessons of self-mastery.

Take paper and pen in hand, and write a list of the things you have done in the past that you feel were mistakes. For example, "I left a good job." "I married the wrong person." "I didn't finish college." "I went out with the wrong crowd." "I missed an opportunity to earn more money." There may be ten or twenty things on your list.

When you are finished, close your eyes and relax. Think of one thing on your list, and remember the circumstances surrounding that particular event in your life. Why did you make that decision? Look at the whole situation with 360-degree vision. What was your mind-set at the time? Were you vulnerable? Were you confused? Who was involved? Did this person influence you? When you have looked at this situation from all angles, do you see any meaning in the "mistake"? What did you learn? How did you survive it?

Then in your mind's eye put that situation in a balloon. There is a string attached to the balloon, and the other end is attached to a part of your body. As the balloon begins to float away, the string pops off, and the situation that you have been holding on to goes with it. You feel a sense of relief. As the balloon soars into the heavens, it begins to fade from sight. Take in a breath and say, "I release my past." Know that this "mistake" is no longer attached to you, and you are free to go on with your life in a new way.

Do as many situations as you wish. Then sit in the silence of your own divine energy and know that there are no mistakes, only experiences that expand your soul and make you the person you are. You always can come back to your list at another time. When you have completed all the things on your list, tear it up and throw it away.

*F*ear can have a paralyzing effect on your life. You feel uncertain, limited, and powerless. Your fear actually pushes away the thing you want. If you need help, ask for it. There are many healers, spiritual teachers, and counselors who are willing to encourage you to face your fears and to guide you to a productive life.

❧ Confronting Fears ❧

When we persist in thoughts of fear, we create a powerful energy force, and we attract the very thing we
fear. When you confront the thought head on, you
actually can release the fear behind it. By recognizing
your fear, you stop giving it any more power over you.

In the silence of your meditation, ask yourself,
"Why am I afraid?" Is the answer unclear? Be persistent.
Ask for a specific reason. Then ask the fear, "What do
you want from me?" Wait for the answer. You may not
want to hear it. Maybe you are a fearful person in
general. Maybe fear keeps you from following your
dreams or taking responsibility for your actions.

Next, picture yourself sitting in a box with your

fear. You cannot escape this box because the fear is keeping you locked inside. There must be a way out of this box of your own making. Look outside the box and notice how different it is out there. Outside the box is freedom. You reach into your pocket and find a key. What is the key? This key will unlock the box. What does the key represent? Is it a change in a belief about yourself or someone else? If so, what would the new thought or belief be? Does it represent a change in your living situation? Do you have to say good-bye to someone who causes you turmoil?

Use your key now, and open the box. Step outside and feel the freedom. By confronting your fear, you have reclaimed your power. The situation and/or the person no longer has a hold on you. The fear is inside the box. You can walk away from it and feel how wonderful it is to be free of this burden. You have changed for the positive and are ready to enjoy all that life has to offer.

There is a tremendous spiritual deficit in the world today. When we continually live in fear, anger, and hatred, we attract situations that will create even more fear, anger, and hatred. The more we involve ourselves in the consciousness of the physical world, the less spiritually in sync we feel.

Take a moment to sense your emotional disturbances. What do you want to say but feel you can't? What are you hiding from? What do you feel depressed about? Why are you always angry? Are you guilt-ridden about something? What are your emotional limitations? Think of some upset that is bothering you right now. If you struggle against your negative emotions, you give them strength. Right now acknowledge your upset. Look at it for what it is. You cannot create the positive without exploring the negative. What in you feels incomplete or out of control that makes you feel so distressed? Can you imagine a different reaction to this upsetting situation? Can you be calm instead of angry?

Ultimately, you are responsible for how you react to a situation.

Imagine that you are a mighty tree in a beautiful garden. The leaves and the branches of the tree represent your emotions and memories. Some of the leaves are just sprouting, and some are withered and ready to fall off. Every leaf is there for a reason, as every emotion is in you for a reason. Acknowledge the negative as well as the positive.

Just as it is natural for leaves to fall and wither, it is natural for your emotions to come and go. You don't have to judge your emotional experiences or hang on to them. Let them go. The tree knows exactly what to do to grow and flourish. It can live for a thousand years. A tree's branches extend far into the world around it. When a wind storm occurs, it bends its branches so they won't break. If one of its branches is diseased, it will break and fall off into the soil to be recycled.

Like this tree, become aware of your enormous energy. Feel the energy all around you. Feel yourself a part of life like this great tree that is constantly changing with the seasons. Like the tree, your body, emotions, and situations are constantly changing. The tree does not try to control how it will grow. It grows naturally as God intended. Know that you, like the tree, are alive and natural, growing as God intended.

*A*ny form of self-condemnation is unnatural to the soul. Guilt especially creates disharmony and causes ailments and illness in our physical bodies.

❧ Good-bye to Guilt ❧

The past is always a teacher for the present. When you feel guilty, you hold on to the past with expectations that something should have been this way or that. You have to free yourself from the overbearing grip of guilt and self-condemnation through forgiveness. That is the only way you can move on.

As you go deeper into your awareness, visualize a truck with the word GUILT emblazoned on its side. All the cargo in this truck is your guilt. You have been carrying it around for a long time. Look inside the truck. What do you still feel guilty about? The experiences come to mind quickly as you gaze inside the truck.

Take a deep breath and become aware of your

heart center. Imagine a ribbon of green light emerging from it. This green healing light of love is surrounding those *guilty pictures* that have been gripping your heart. Send out a thought of forgiveness to anyone or any scenario about which you still feel guilty. Continue to send light and forgiveness to anyone and anything that has caused you to feel guilty until you feel the guilt diminish. Look inside the truck once again. Has the load been lightened? Is the truck half full or nearly empty?

Next, see yourself standing in front of a mirror and viewing your image. Concentrate on your heart center and the healing green light that emanates from it. It surrounds your entire body. Say to yourself, *"I forgive myself for . . ."* (fill in the rest). Take another deep breath and become aware of a new forgiving consciousness you are forming all around your energy field.

You are on this Earth to learn, and learning comes in a variety of ways with different people and situations. When you live with guilt and are unwilling to forgive yourself, you stop learning. Let this be a new day and a new awareness with forgiveness in your heart for you.

Often in our desire to be loved, we try so hard to be everything to everyone. We compromise our true selves in an expectation to please someone else. If we continue to live for the approval of others, we will find ourselves unhappy about life and unfulfilled in our own dreams. We can never be truly happy until we live our own lives.

Be Balanced in All Things

Think of how it feels to stand on one leg for any length of time. After a few moments, you are leaning one way or another, feeling as if you're going to fall. It is easy to get out of balance in your life—emotionally, mentally, and spiritually—especially if you try to do too much or live according to other people's standards.

With your eyes closed, see or sense yourself in a garden. Look around. Is there orderliness in your garden, or do you see a lot of weeds or vines overtaking the flowers in your garden? Are the flowers in bloom, or have some of them died? Do you see overgrown bushes or plants? The weeds, vines, dead flowers, and overgrown bushes represent people and situations that are either taking over your life or draining your energy. They are causing you to be out of balance.

Observe your garden once again. Is there anything missing? Are there dirt piles where nothing is growing? As you sit in the silence of your meditation, ask yourself: "What can I do to make things different?" Is there someone you need to let go of in your life? Is there a situation that you have been ignoring that needs handling? The answers are there inside you. You don't have to ask anyone else.

Take a moment and begin to see your garden in a new light. What a difference! The flowers are blooming, the weeds have been cleared away, and the plants are nicely trimmed. Your new garden is beautiful, lush, and green. Know that like your garden, your life is taking shape and coming into balance. You can return here any time to trim away the excess or clear out the unwanted.

You must begin to take responsibility for your life. You do have the power to control what you think and how you react to a situation.

❧ A Positive You ❧

Are you someone who is always waiting for the other shoe to drop? Something good happens, but then you believe something bad is coming next. You have to change this negative picture of life if you want to have long-lasting harmony and happiness. If you expect the worst, you'll get it. You must begin to see yourself in a new light, one that is positive, enthusiastic, and expecting the good to happen.

In your relaxed state, imagine you are sitting in a movie theater. You are the only one there. The lights are dim, and the movie is about to begin. From the first roll of credits, you realize that the movie is your life on screen. There you are as a baby coming into the world. Was it a happy birth? If it wasn't pleasant, you have the power right now to edit that scene. You can make it a happy birth. Let yourself feel good about coming into this particular incarnation. The scenes move along into your childhood. Are you playing with your friends? Are you being scolded by a parent? Are you alone and afraid? Whatever the picture, change it to a positive scene. See yourself as you wish to be. Feel how you want to be treated. Edit any negative situations out, so that you feel good about your childhood. It is a childhood filled with love and good times.

The movie continues, and you watch a scene from your teen years. Again, if it is a negative situation, you can edit the scene and make it better. It's your movie, and you have the power to change what you don't like. You're in charge. Replace the scene with something you would like to see. Feel how happy you are now that the scene is one that you like. If good things occurred in your life, focus on these scenes and reinforce the happy feelings that you once felt. It's important that you feel good in this process.

Now you're an adult. All those happy, good feelings are still inside you. If there is a situation in the present that is making you miserable or stressed, you are the person in charge, so you can edit that scene to your satisfaction. You are very creative and powerful. See the new scene as you want it to be. Be willing to let go of your fixed ideas. Replace fear with love and harmony. Practice changing your inner pictures, and give yourself control over your own life. As you sit there in the movie theater of your mind, let those good feelings stay with you.

How do we recognize the power of God within us? The quickest way is to tear down the walls of self-criticism and self-judgment and nurture ourselves with love. Then we begin to live in the realm of possibilities and promise.

❧ *Love Yourself* ❧

As you relax in the rhythm of your breath, envision your special place or sanctuary. It may be a garden or waterfall or meadow. This is the place in your mind's eye where you feel safe, secure, and at peace.

Sit or lie down in this special place, and begin to feel even more relaxed and at one with all of life. Turn your attention to the area around your heart. This is your center of unconditional love. See this area being filled by a beautiful pink light of love. Any tightness around this area is alleviated. The healing light of love is clearing all the old hurts and pains that have been stored in here. Continue to let this beautiful pink light mend and repair feelings of hurt. As it does, visualize the area around your heart expand with love and compassion. Let this center fill with as much healing energy as you can possibly imagine.

Next, encircle yourself with this wonderful pink healing light of love. Let this energy absorb all your doubts and fears so that you feel clear and free of them. Let this light fill your whole being with unconditional love. No matter what you have said or done to yourself in the past, this pink light absorbs it until it is gone. Any time you need to love who you are, you can return to your sanctuary and use this pink healing light to expand your heart center.

The more we let go of the ego, the more room there is for our divinity to shine through. We become mindful of the unity in all things. Our consciousness expands, and exciting insights come to mind. When we step into our divine self, we are opened up to the many choices and opportunities that our soul provides.

✤ Let Go of Ego ✤

Self-esteem is knowing that you are worthwhile. When we base our decisions on ego and not on self-worth, we are doing something out of fear and inadequacy. The ego is the "i," which is not the same as the "I" of the spiritual self. When we try to control everything from the "i," we block the flow of energy from spirit. We must learn to blend the ego with the higher aspects of our being and bring ourselves into balance.

As you close your eyes, take several deep breaths into your body and the space around you. Repeat to yourself, "I open myself to what the universe wants to show me. I step out of my way and let it be." In your mind's eye, envision yourself sitting in the center of the universe. As you continue to take deep breaths, notice the galaxies and stars around you. You become aware of the moon and planets. Your vision expands to see the Milky Way and beyond—worlds that seem to go on forever. There is a light that spreads throughout the universe formed by millions upon millions of shining stars. You understand that you are one speck among millions, and at the same time you are a part of this great infinity of life. The more you realize that you are a part of something so big, the more you let go of your small self. As the universe is limitless, so you, too, are unlimited. You are an integral part of this universe. Without you, everything is out of sync. You are a necessary part of the natural order of the universe.

As you exhale, release all your criticism, complaining, fear, and expectations. You don't have to control life. You are a universal being among other universal beings. You trust that the universe will send whatever you need and want. You know there is a limitless source of good at your disposal. With your arms wide open in acceptance, you see your good coming your way. You feel good about your place in the universe. You know that you are a necessary part of the whole. With this knowledge, you feel calm and clear. Your ego and spirit are balanced and ready for new and exciting possibilities.

When we love ourselves, we live in a state of God consciousness. This is living in heaven while walking upon the earth. In this state, we are prepared to take part in the fruits of our spiritual heritage.

Your Power Symbol

As you sit in the quiet of your meditative state, become aware of your infinite power. This power is a divine source of immense good. It does not judge or hold grudges. It is unconditional love. Envision this infinite power as a symbol. It can be a star or millions of stars, a sunburst, or a religious figure like Buddha or Christ. Know that this sacred symbol represents your power. Because this power is a part of you, you have the ability to create your life and your environment the way you want.

Is there is a person, place, situation, or circumstance that is currently holding you back? If so, see it now. Ask yourself, "Why is this in my life? What am I learning from this person or this situation? What is the origin of these negative charges inside me? Is it my own fear, or someone else's?"

Envision your sacred power symbol in front of you. Feel its energy of strength and goodwill. Replay the same scene, and with your power symbol, eliminate the limiting factor and replace it with the element of love. Notice how different the scene becomes. Something has changed.

As you sit in the center of your power, feel confident that you can draw into your life only those experiences that are for your highest good and spiritual development. Let your power symbol become one with every choice you make from now on. When in doubt, visualize your symbol, and let its positive energy guide you along your path of a new day and new choices. Know deep down that you have the power of your sacred energy alive inside you. It is through this infusion of the God energy that you feel self-assured and strong.

When you meditate, you are spending precious time with your Higher Self. The Higher Self is the connection between your physical personality and the divine energy that flows through everything and everyone. The more you are in tune with your Higher Self, the more you become aware of the light being that you are.

❧ Your Direction in Life ❧

One of the ways we feel confident about life is knowing we have a direction. When we walk through life without goals and interest, we are like sheep wandering mindlessly. We follow the path of others instead of our own path. Know that you are here to take your own road, no matter what others may say or do. Traveling down your own path in life will make all the difference.

As you sit in the silence of your own divine center, imagine that you are on a road in the woods. Around you are glorious trees and fresh-smelling fields of flowers. On the other side of the hill you can hear the din of traffic noise. People are scattered here and there. Some are walking; others are riding in cars.

As you continue to walk, you stop at a fork in the road. You look in both directions. You wonder if there will be too many people or a lot of traffic on one road. You wonder if you will be lonely on the other. Which is the right road for you? You call to your Higher Self saying *"Help me make the right decision."* Immediately your heart center lights up. You look again at the two roads. One road seems to be in need of repair from so much traffic. There are potholes and patches every few feet. The other road seems smoother and less bumpy with some grassy spots, but it has more curves than the other. Way off in the distance, there is a point where you can see both roads converge.

In the stillness of your heart center, you choose the path that is right for you. You are happy with your decision. You feel a quiet confidence in choosing this particular road. No matter the twists and turns, it will lead you home. You take a step forward . . . you are on your way. You feel you are on the path to your true destiny. You have direction now. You know where you are going.

Whenever doubt arises, picture this fork in the road and the choice you have made. Know, too, that your Higher Self is with you. You have made the right choice.

*W*hen you tune in to intuition, you are in touch with your sixth sense or psychic awareness. Intuition is subtle. It is not an outside force that compels you, but rather a small inner voice that knows.

❦ Tuning In to Intuition ❧

To develop your intuition, you must open the channels of psychic energy that travel up and down your spine in the seven main energy centers called chakras. These chakras appear as spinning wheels of light that vibrate in different colors. If these centers are blocked, you cannot receive clear intuitive messages.

In your meditative state, focus your attention on the very bottom of your spine. This is your root chakra. Imagine it is a fiery furnace churning up a very vital red energy. This is the fire of life. Use all your imagination to feel how hot this energy is. Then visualize this energy moving in a clockwise direction as it builds up your physical energy. You feel the strength of this red energy. Allow this hot, fiery energy to encircle your lower body to your feet. This energy is essential in the development of your psychic awareness.

Turn the furnace up and see the flame rise up your body into the second chakra located just below your navel. This is the area of sexuality and creativity. The red flame becomes an orange light. You can feel a slight difference in energy as this orange spinning wheel of light encircles this area of your body.

Now return to the fiery furnace, and let the red energy move into the orange light and go even higher. As it enters the solar plexus center located above your navel, the area turns into a brilliant yellow color. This is the seat of your intuition, where gut reactions and feelings are stored. This is the area where you first receive impressions. As the yellow light spins around, the sensitivity in this area increases. Your intuitive feelings become more intense.

Return to the root chakra, and visualize that red energy moving up your body once again, through the orange, then yellow, until you reach the heart center, where it blends into a beautiful green light. This is the area of unconditional love and compassion. Concentrate and expand this center with as much green light as you can. You can use this green, healing light to help others as well as yourself.

Again return to the furnace and bring the red energy up the energy centers. See it blend into the orange, then yellow, then green spinning wheels of light. It moves up into the throat center, and the color becomes a vibrant cobalt blue. This fifth chakra is the center of clairaudience, or clear hearing. As this light glows brighter and stronger in your throat chakra, your ability to hear spirit speak to you increases.

Remember that you have an unlimited supply of energy. Return to the root center, and bring up the red energy into all the chakras until it merges into the third eye center in the middle of your forehead. This is the center of clairvoyance, or clear seeing. To develop your gift of clairvoyance, concentrate on this center. Feel the energy in this center. You might receive flashes of scenes and symbols in this center.

Once again, return to the root chakra, and churn the energy up through all the chakra centers until you reach the top of your head and your crown chakra. A burst of violet flame emerges. This center is the doorway to the spiritual realms. Through this violet flame, you channel spiritual and cosmic energy. As the violet light grows brighter, the flames radiate from this center, getting higher until they merge with the golden light of the heaven worlds. See this golden light going back through your body and down through your energy centers. The golden light swirls around and fills your body. As it spills out the top of your head, you feel illuminated and protected. Your intuition is now open and ready to receive information.

When you are open to life, you create an energy force that says yes. It's amazing how much good is waiting to come into your life. Yesterday has passed and tomorrow has yet to come. The only time is right now. Trust in the process of life.

Trust the Guidance from Within

By learning to trust yourself and your feelings, you are attuning yourself to the power of your soul awareness. We are always walking with the God force energy, and the more we attune ourselves to this force, the more we can trust ourselves to make the right decisions in our lives.

In the quiet of your inner sanctuary, think about a decision you recently made. Did you trust your very first instinct with the situation or not? Did your choice originate from a place of love or one of fear? You need to be honest with yourself when you do this exercise. Take an inventory of your life, including your loved ones, your friends, your job, your home, and your money. Are they the results of your trusting that inner voice, or were they made from ego? Were you afraid of hurting someone's feelings, or were you too vain to tell the truth? Do you live your life based on other people's belief systems and other people's fears?

As you sit quietly, in tune with your own breathing, focus on your throat chakra. Your inner voice is subtle but grows stronger when you listen. It is a voice of love and peace. This is your voice of truth, and it will never lead you in the wrong direction. It will not always sound logical like your rational mind. The rational mind tries to give you the answer you want to hear. Intuition is not wishing for something. Wishes are based on judgment, opinions, and a desire for something. Intuition just knows. Focus on your throat chakra and listen for spirit.

From this day forward, when you have a choice to make, you are going to trust that still, small voice from within. Always ask, "What's the right choice for me?" Then sit still and listen. Be reassured that your inner voice will never abandon you. When you trust your inner truth, you will always live your life, *not* someone else's.

One of the most tragic and all too common situations I encounter in my work is a spirit coming through with remorse for an unsatisfied life. How much better life could have been if these souls could have expressed their true creative natures and appreciated the many things they accomplished while living on Earth.

The Hole of Self-Doubt and Criticism

When you doubt yourself or criticize your abilities, it's as if you are stuck in a deep hole in the ground. Every time you want to climb up out of the hole, your self-doubt and criticism push you back down. The more you listen to other people's opinions as your truth, the deeper down the hole you go.

Think of some of the doubts that you have had about your talents or abilities in the last year. Has your attitude been helpful, or does it fill you with hopelessness? Have you been on the self-pity train? That kind of attitude will always push you straight down into the hole.

Today is the day that you decide enough is enough. You want to escape this black hole of misery created with your own critical voice. You look around the hole and notice a ladder leaning against the side. You look up and see a circle of light at the top. The ladder represents your unique qualities. You have a lot of creativity inside you, but you have been burying it down this hole. With an acknowledgment of each of your qualities and talents, you take one step up the ladder toward the light. It's the only way up, and you are equipped to get out. Think about each talent and each ability and start climbing.

After a few rungs up, some self-doubt appears. Thank it for showing up, but tell your doubt that you've decided to bypass it. Visualize this doubt fly up and dissipate into the light above. You continue to climb the ladder and are almost at the top. If a criticism pops into mind, again thank it, and tell it to join doubt in the light.

Finally, give yourself one big push past all that "junk" with which you have been criticizing yourself, and emerge victorious out of the hole. The sun is bright. The light of the universe shines its love and admiration upon you. From now on, whenever you criticize yourself or doubt your ability, think of the hole and know that you have conquered it. You stay true to your creative abilities, and release doubt and criticism into the light and move on.

*T*he word "inspiration" means to fill with spirit. *Spirits are always trying to communicate to us. They do so by imposing their thoughts into our consciousness. I call it mind-to-mind communication. Many times we are inspired by spirits to take a particular action. When our psychic centers are open, we become clearer channels for spirit transmission.*

❧ Open to Inspiration ❧

This is a writing exercise, so have a pad or notebook and a pen by your side. Writing is a great tool for freeing the mind to express itself.

Get comfortable. As you follow the rhythm of your breath, become more relaxed and open to your inner voice. Let your thoughts pass through. Don't try to analyze anything. Sit in the silence for a while.

When you open your eyes, begin to write in your notebook. Let your thoughts just pour out on the paper. They have been floating in your mind for the past several minutes, so begin to write them down. If you want, you can write these thoughts as a letter to yourself.

Describe your emotions in colors and pictures. Do you feel gray or bright blue? Do you feel like a doormat or a brick building, a butterfly or an ant? Express yourself in as much colorful detail as you can. Don't analyze any of it. Don't try to make something up. Just listen and write.

Now close your eyes and keep writing. Let spirit come through and impress you with thoughts. Don't think about anything. Open your eyes and continue to write. Is there a difference in the writing from when you first began? Are the thoughts enthusiastic, philosophical, or unexpected? Inspirational thought lacks intense emotional feeling. It is more like stream-of-consciousness writing, filled with impressions and concepts that can be very deep and moving.

This exercise can help to free your mind from everyday, mundane thoughts and inspire you with some creative ideas.

*O*ften we are not aware of how negative energy goes out like ripples on a lake and makes contact with everyone in its path. Your body picks up this stagnant energy, and suddenly your behavior changes. It is important to check your energy on a daily basis and clear all the emotional and mental baggage that you may have picked up.

❧ Clearing Negative Energy ❧

Some of us are "sensitive sponges." We pick up energy pretty easily from family members, friends, and even strangers. This unwanted energy can zap us of vitality, cause or intensify self-destructive patterns, and hinder our healing process. This exercise, which is done in the shower, is excellent if you have been in a lot of emotional turmoil. It will help to clear out all unwanted energy that has been projected on to you by others.

As you stand in the shower, close your eyes and think of the water as cleansing energy that is washing away all the emotional and mental debris of the day. Does anyone come to mind as you do this? Take a breath and let the water wash away the energy. As the water falls on your head, imagine it going through your body like streams of cleansing light. All the negative thought forms are leaving your energy field, exiting your feet, and going down the drain. Continue to envision the water washing away any excess energy that is not yours. As it goes down the drain, you feel lighter and cleaner inside as well as outside. Once all the energy that is not yours is gone, imagine the water filling you up with your own energy. You feel every cell in your body being restored. You feel invigorated and ready for your day.

Negative psychic energy often is attracted to us by our own fearful thoughts and feelings like anger, resentment, envy, and hatred. The way to avoid negative psychic energy is to persist in the positive and let go of depressing thoughts and unkind attitudes.

A Shield of Protection

This is another meditation that can help to clear your energy field as well as protect you from any unwanted and uncomfortable psychic vibrations.

Start with the grounding exercise. Enter your sanctuary and stand there. Visualize a small hand vacuum or a hose attached to a vacuum cleaner. Start at the top of your head and begin to vacuum away any images or feelings that are there. You can see all that energy going up the hose like dust. Vacuum your whole body. If your vacuum bag gets full, throw it out or blow it up, and get a new vacuum bag. Clean every spot in your energy field down to your feet. As you clear your space, you will begin to feel lighter and brighter. When you're finished, blow up your vacuum, and know that all the energy is disposed of and gone from you.

Now imagine a wall of protection around you. This can be a shield of light around you or a glass box in which you place yourself. It can look like an invisible blanket or cloak of protective energy. Whatever it is, imagine that it is made of light and love. No one can penetrate your space unless you give him or her permission. You are always in control of your energy field. As you seal this light around you, focus your thoughts on love, so that what you send out to others will not harm or hurt them. Let only your love go out so that love will come back.

*S*ome people are psychic vampires: They siphon off your energy, and you feel completely incapacitated. Many of these people vibrate at low-frequency levels. You can feel this low vibration, but you may not know what it is. Intuitively, you feel uncomfortable or anxious.

✎ The Cone of Light ✎

Here is a simple exercise you can do if you are confronted by a negative person or are in a situation where you feel upset, afraid, or exhausted. Usually this means that your energy is being quickly depleted.

Wherever you are, take a moment and close your eyes. Focus on your heart center. Feel yourself enveloped with the healing green light of this psychic center. Then imagine a cone of light dropping down on each side of your body until you are surrounded by light. Concentrate on being completely sealed off from the energy of the person, room, or situation. As you concentrate, the light around you will deflect any negative vibrations being hurled in your direction. Imagine any negative energy bouncing off the cones of light and returning to its sender. If you concentrate like this for a few minutes, you will begin to notice a change in the atmosphere around you. Usually the person causing the emotional turmoil or negativity will stop what he or she is doing or leave the room altogether.

*W*e always have spirit guides around us, and they impress our thoughts with the higher qualities of life such as patience, humility, acceptance, confidence, joy, and humor. Usually we have one master guide that stays with us throughout our life and sometimes through many lifetimes. Some people refer to this guide as a guardian angel. To me, spirit guides and angels are the same.

✑ Meeting Your Spirit Guide ✑

Spirit guides are highly evolved beings that are a source of expertise to us. As a medium, I am always working with my guides to disseminate information in the best possible way to my clients. Our guides are always around us; some for a long time, others for a particular purpose and then they leave. This meditation will help you to contact your master guide.

In your relaxed state, enter your sanctuary. Take a moment to familiarize yourself with everything in your sanctuary. Awaken your senses here, so that you not only can see, but hear, smell, and feel everything in this place. This is where you will come to talk and to work with your spirit guides and teachers.

Use your thoughts and ask that your master guide stand in front of you so that you can see him or her. This may take a while the first time. Notice your guide's physical traits, such as hair, eyes, clothing, and anything else that distinguishes him or her. Don't judge what comes to you. Keep your focus on love. A master guide is one with whom we have a close affinity. He or she can appear in particular garments that will seem familiar or will seem to be from a certain period in time.

When you are ready, ask your guide questions. You can begin with: "Who are you? How do you work with me? What is your mission for me?" On subsequent visits with your guide, you can ask questions relating to specific circumstances in your life: "What shall I do about so and so? Is this job right for me?"

Become aware of your guide's response. Is it a picture? Is it a scent? Does your guide whisper to you? Pay attention to all your senses. You are communicating between the worlds. You may feel your whole energy field change as you commune with your guide. Sometimes the information from your guide may not come immediately, but it will come through in the future as an idea.

As you meditate and become more attuned to the subtle energy around you, you will draw your guide closer to you. The more you persevere in this practice, the more you will become aware of your guide's influence, wisdom, and higher energy vibration.

*A*lways question your guide. Let your guide give you a sign or a symbol, such as a butterfly or a yellow rose, with which to validate his or her presence. If this symbol shows up in your life in the next week or so, you will have confirmation. If not, then try again, perhaps several times. You have to practice elevating your energy so that you can communicate clearly with your guide.

❧ Spiritual Protection ❧

We have many spirit guides who come in and out of our lives at certain periods of time. A protector guide's main purpose is to protect your space from any energies that might cause you harm. This guide is important especially when you are in a crisis or feeling despair, depressed, fearful, or anxious.

When you are relaxed and grounded, enter your sanctuary and ask that your protector guide come forward. This guide is like a gatekeeper at the door to your soul. Make sure that you work from love and not fear. It is important that you know if a guide is a highly evolved being or another entity. You always want to ask that any being that comes to you is for your highest good. Ask for it to enter in the light of God.

Ask your protector guide to stand by you so that you feel the strength of its presence. Sometimes a protector guide can be a powerful animal, such as a lion or bear. Pay attention to your thoughts. Your guide may impress you with thoughts of encouragement. If you do not see or hear your guide, you may *sense* a confidence within yourself. This self-assurance is what you need at this moment. Focus on love and have faith in your abilities. Surround yourself with light. Know that this guide is here to assist you with strength and courage and is with you every step of the way. In your hour of need, your guide will never abandon you.

The normal state of the body is health. When we are experiencing illness, energy is blocked, depleted, or scattered. The electromagnetic field of energy that surrounds you is composed of many layers of light, color, and sound. This energy field accumulates every thought, word, feeling, and action of your life.

Tuning In to Your Healing

As you sit with your eyes closed, become aware of your body. Imagine the energy of the body soaring up and down your spine. As you open to your sensitivity, inhale and hold the breath for the count of four, and imagine the golden white light of the cosmos penetrating the top of your head. This cosmic light travels to the parts of your body that are in pain. Exhale on the count of four and let go of the pain. Imagine it exiting through your mouth as a gray mist. Continue this breathing exercise until you feel your pain lessening or completely gone.

Next envision your entire body enclosed in a bubble. As this bubble floats up to the ceiling, it rises out the roof of your home. As you sit in the bubble, you can see your neighborhood below, including houses, roadways, and all the activity along the way. The bubble transports you to a beautiful park lined with trees and flower beds. You can smell the perfumed air of roses, lavender, and lilac. The bubble descends and lands gently on the grass.

You step outside your bubble and sit on a marble bench. Everything seems so vibrant and alive. It is time to create your perfectly healthy body. As the cosmic golden light from the heavens enters your body, it merges with the natural energies of your physical body. You begin to let go of everything that keeps you from feeling good.

Starting at the base of your spine, the cosmic energy blends with the red energy of the root chakra to bring aliveness and vitality to your body. This red energy stimulates your circulation and removes any blockages from your blood. The red passes through the adrenal glands, dissipating any worry, and you feel much more relaxed. Any fatigue that you have been feeling is gone.

The cosmic energy moves into the spleen chakra,

causing the orange light to travel up and down your body, stimulating your mental functions. Your courage is strengthened and your inhibitions are dissolved. This light surrounds your kidneys, gall bladder, and spleen, correcting what is necessary to bring them to proper functioning.

The cosmic light moves next into the solar plexus center right above your belly button and intermingles with the yellow light of this chakra. This psychic center affects your nervous system, so it brings a calming to your nerves. The digestion and elimination processes of your colon, intestine, and liver are all properly balanced and purified.

As the cosmic energy moves into your heart, you feel an optimism as the green light merges with the cosmic forces. It opens your sense of love and peace. If you have blood pressure or heart problems, the green ray of energy dissolves any inadequacies and brings healing. Emotional problems are neutralized. The faces of people who have been tugging at your heart are surrounded by the cosmic energy, and you feel safe and comfortable.

As you visualize the throat area, the blue light

emerges. Your sense of self-expression is opened. You are able to communicate easily and be more yourself. Your creative abilities are unlocked and free to take charge. The cosmic energy moves up into your third eye, and the indigo ray purifies your vision and disperses your fears. If you have had been any head trauma or mental problems, the indigo light soothes this area and corrects any imperfections.

At the top of your head the violet flame mingles with golden white light and opens the doorway to your spiritual enlightenment. Any nervous conditions, tumors, rheumatism, bladder problems are enveloped by this violet light, so they can be healed. You feel so much better than before.

Visualize yourself in your everyday situations. People are commenting that you look so well. You smile and know it's true. Your health has been restored, and you feel energized. Know that this healing energy is at work in your body. Each day you feel stronger and healthier.

*W*hen you create a radiant energy field through thoughts of love, respect, and kindheartedness, people will naturally be attracted to you. Your mere presence can be a healing force for everyone with whom you come into contact.

✺ X-Ray Vision ✺

We live in a world where constant levels of stress and worry are common. This excess energy usually lodges in the area around your head. To me it appears like static electricity or electrical sparks shooting out the top of the head. If you don't clear the energy, you are susceptible to all types of problems, such as headaches, colds, insomnia, depression, and sinus and allergy conditions, to name a few. This exercise will help to balance the excessive energy and restore that which has been depleted.

In your mind's eye, imagine that you are standing in front of an X-ray machine. Above your head is the healing cosmic light. This light is going to scan your energy field and heal the imbalances. Begin by pushing the button on the X-ray machine. Your whole body is illuminated with light. Look at everything in your body and your entire energy field. If there are black, brownish, or gray areas, shine the light on these places until they are neutralized and normal once more. As you do, say to yourself, "I am the light of God."

If you see any cracks, openings, or leaks where your energy is being siphoned or is draining out, once again you shine the light on these areas and seal them closed. Repeat the affirmation, "I am the light of God."

If you see any faces superimposed in any area of your body, such as your back, neck, heart, throat, or legs, shine the light on these parts. You may see shadows or figures in these areas that could be relatives, friends, coworkers, or even strangers. Let the light saturate these images until they are dissolved. Say again, "I am the light of God."

Look over your entire body once more through the X-ray machine and check for anything else that may be unhealthy or out of place. Repair any holes or gaps with light, so that everything is perfectly sealed. Then encase your whole body in light, and repeat: "I am the light of God."

Before we are born, we decide many things with our spirit guides. We pick our gender, parents, the relationships we want to experience, our sexual orientation, our place, time, and station in life, and even the cause of our death. Our choices always are made with free will and reflect the spiritual work we want to accomplish.

❧ Balance Your Sexual Energy ❧

Many of us judge ourselves by our sex and our sexuality to the point that we let it become far too important. Sex is a wonderful part of who we are, and we can express it joyfully and in a balanced way. If you have been placing too much emphasis on sex, you might need to rebalance the energy and bring it to other parts of the body where there may be deficiencies.

Close your eyes and imagine that you are a flower bulb planted in the earth. As the sunlight touches the dirt, the energy in the bulb begins to generate, and a stem sprouts through the earth. See your feet as the bulb and your legs as the stem. There is a life energy force rising up the stem, and out of it emerges the buds of a flower. These buds are your torso. As the flower petals open, you feel this energy move into your neck and head.

Imagine the stem rising higher, the petals opening into full bloom, and the life energy force expressing its beauty as an exquisite flower. This is you with all your energy intact. Envision the flower of your choice: a rose, a daffodil, a tulip, a gardenia. See its size, shape, and color. Smell its wonderful fragrance. No perfume can surpass the aroma of this flower. This flower represents you as a totally balanced being. Watch as the flower bends toward the light of the sun for warmth, protection, and life. Feel the forces of life express themselves in all parts of your body. You are fully alive!

$\mathcal{W}$e are here to accept ourselves and others with love and compassion. If we could learn this one thing, we would feel more content and enjoy our time on earth. We could throw away our bottles of Prozac, or alcohol, or whatever numbs us, because we would feel able to handle whatever came our way.

✍ A Healing Atmosphere ✍

In order to heal yourself, it is important to nurture yourself in every way and create a healing atmosphere within and around you.

When you are relaxed, in your mind's eye, float up to the ceiling and look at yourself sitting in the chair. You want to get a different perspective—a higher perspective. Look at your physical appearance. Do you look tired or anxious? Have you been getting enough rest, or have you been running around a lot taking care of this thing and that one? From your higher perspective, look at what you may need to nurture yourself more. Is it a better diet, more exercise, a night out with your friends, or more quiet time?

You can ask your spirit guides to help you. Together you and your guides send a beautiful violet and white light to surround the person sitting there in the chair. This light will quicken your vibration to resonate with the higher frequencies. Envision your guides as they concentrate on you with their thoughts of love and light. All tension, aches, and pain are dissolving in this love. You feel your body freed of its burdens as it continues to be bathed in this healing atmosphere of love and light.

You realize that you are never alone even if sometimes you are unaware. As you feel more peaceful and relaxed, you have a greater understanding and compassion for yourself. When you are ready, return to your body in the chair and awaken with a new, healthy consciousness. This awareness is yours from this moment on.

*M*ost relationships fall apart because of our lack of awareness. Instead of harboring ill will toward the other person, we can choose to look at it from an honest perspective. If we cannot get beyond our own anger and resentment, we will repeat the situation in other relationships until we learn its lesson.

Let Go of Heartache

As you become more relaxed, focus on your heart center. This is the area where you hold on to lost loves, grief over loss, and sorrow for what might have been. As you focus, ask your spirit guides and loved ones on the other side to assist you in releasing the wounds that have cut deeply.

As you bridge the gap between worlds, imagine your spirit guides and other loved ones gathering around you. The light shines from each one of them as they send loving thoughts of kindness and gentleness your way. Let their love enter your heart. See this energy break up and disperse any feelings of anger, resentment, fear, and pain you may have there.

Continue to let these thoughts of love penetrate this area until you feel all the negative energy disintegrate into tiny particles and leave your body through your fingertips and toes. See this energy traveling into the universe and dissolving into the heavens.

Listen for any messages from your guides or loved ones. Are they telling you that things will be better? The more you release your sorrow and pain, the more you can see clearly the reason for this change in the relationship. What is the lesson? Do you need to be more self-reliant? Do you need to take care of your needs more than someone else's? Do you need to let go of jealousy? Do you need to be more spontaneous and not as controlling? Whatever the lesson, your heart is now free to receive the information. You sit quietly and patiently until the message is apparent. Take in a deep breath. You feel so relieved.

Your loved ones and spirit guides are smiling. They continue to send their light and love your way. When you are ready to open your eyes, you will find that you feel so much better. A heavy burden has been lifted off your heart. You feel ready for a new chapter in your life to begin.

When we begin to recognize the light of love within ourselves, it is easier to see that light in others. When two people are in love, they see that light in each other's eyes. The world outside does not exist for them because they are in a private world of love and feel the splendor and joy that love bestows.

✍ A Loving Relationship ✍

Visualize the inside of a theater. You are the only member of the audience. The show is about to begin, and it's a new romantic comedy. This is not just any show, this is *your* show. You are the producer, writer, and lead player. You have a program in your hand. As you look at it, a title that best describes the loving relationship you would like to experience appears on the front cover. One or two words come to mind immediately. Maybe it's an entire phrase. Once you have a title, open the program. The cast is listed. You are the star, so you are the main character. What is the description of your character? Acknowledge the positive and negative traits you possess, those that your character will demonstrate.

Once you have finished your character's description, it is time to create the other lead actor. Visualize physical traits—height, weight, hair color, and so forth. Give this character the attributes you want, and be as specific as possible. Is the person humorous, generous, kind, candid, punctual, and neat? Visualize this leading character rehearsing each one of the traits until he or she has all of them down pat.

The lights dim, and you look up. The curtain opens; Act I begins. It is a scene in the day in the life of the character representing you. Visualize as much detail as possible in order to get your story across. The curtain comes down at the end of this act. You are enjoying the play thus far. It is time for Act II. This is where the second character makes an entrance. Play this scene in a variety of possibilities until one in particular fits best. Remember, as the writer, you are in control of how the play turns out. The curtain descends, and this act is over.

Act III begins. This is the grand finale where the two main characters fall deeply in love. Visualize each one expressing their love, respect, and admiration for the other. It's magical. Of course your play has a wonderful ending. The two main characters live happily ever after. The curtain comes down. You are feeling very contented and hopeful. You look forward to the new relationship that is about to come into your life.

When we act with compassion, peace, and dignity in our relationships, we are expressing an illuminated spirit. Seek to express strength, goodwill, love, and courage so that your light can shine through you and illuminate others.

~ Understanding Others ~

Imagine that you are on your cell phone. On the other end is a person whom you need to better understand. Visualize yourself holding the phone to your ear as you listen to the other person's phone ringing. The person answers, "Hello." In your mind you respond: "Hi, I wanted to call you because I feel as if I don't fully understand something about you." Then talk about some situation that needs clarification. "What did you mean when you said . . . ?" Fill in the problem that is troubling you. Then listen. You can hear the person on the other end explaining to you about the situation or circumstance.

If you hear static when the person is talking or

don't fully comprehend the message, interrupt and request that he or she slow down and speak more clearly. "What is your true motivation?" you ask. When the person communicates this time, the meaning behind the misunderstanding becomes more evident. You begin to have a better picture of this individual and can begin to see the situation in a different light.

If more explanation is needed, the next step of this communication is to ask the person to show you visually what you do not fully comprehend. Then look at the screen on your cell phone and see the person acting out the scenario so that it becomes quite obvious to you. You may have to spend some minutes seeing the situation on the screen until it becomes crystal clear. With your new understanding, you feel better about this person and the whole situation.

*S*ometimes tragedies, such as the death of a child or a long-term illness, even disasters involving thousands of people, are difficult to understand with our earthly minds. When we come to the realization that a soul always makes the choice to go through a particular experience, no matter how bad it seems, we can more easily accept that certain situations cannot be controlled or changed.

∽ The Doorway Home ∽

Many of us have a difficult time letting go and saying good-bye when someone we love dies. Saying good-bye is a way for the mind to realize that the person is gone physically; it does not dismiss the person or end the opportunity to speak to him or her again. We must remember that our loved ones never die; they have shed their physical bodies and have made a transition from one dimension to another.

Begin this meditation by entering your sanctuary. You can sit on a bench or under a tree or on the sand of a beautiful beach. Then imagine your loved one coming to you. This person is no longer ill, or old, or in pain, but rather quite healthy and at an age he or she once enjoyed on Earth. If a child passed over, the child may come to you as a teen or a young adult because children keep growing in the spirit realms.

Envision your loved one as whole and happy, perhaps wearing a favorite suit or outfit. Imagine the scent of the perfume she wore or a particular activity he enjoyed. Picture in your mind as many details as you can. Your loved one sits next to you, and you both enjoy the peaceful atmosphere. You begin to ask questions about your loved one's experience on the other side: *"How do you feel? What is it like where you are?"* The answers come to you. *Be at peace. I am alive. There is no reason to worry. I have come to show you that there is no death.*

Now it's your turn to express yourself and whatever you may be feeling. If there is something you wanted to tell your loved one but didn't have the chance, say it now. Give yourself time to express your feelings.

Once you reveal your feelings, your mind is flooded with all the wonderful experiences you shared together. These memories fill your mind with love. You hug your loved one, assured that he or she is safe and at home in new surroundings.

Your loved one then hands you a golden box encased with sparkling jewels. Every memory, thought, word, and deed you shared together is contained in this box. When you open it, the love flows out like ribbons of white and gold light. The love fills your heart. Love can never die. This box is a reminder that your loved one is always with you, no longer in pain, but perfect in spirit. *I'll see you in your dreams.*

The time comes when you must say good-bye. You know that you must release your loved one so that he or she can continue the journey in the spirit realm. You also realize that your work on Earth is not finished, so you must return to your reality. As you take in a deep breath, you feel calm and reassured that your loved one is safe. You also understand that one day your turn will come, and when it does, your loved ones will be there to greet you as you cross over to the other side. They will take you by the hand, and together you will return home to heaven.

*L*oss is a natural part of life. Something is born, and something dies. It takes time to get through the grieving process. By accepting your feelings and moving through them, you can begin to pick up the pieces of your life and go on.

Healing Your Loss

You may want to have a pad and pen by your side to jot down the information that comes to mind. Allow yourself to relax by imagining all parts of your body becoming limp and comfortable. Let a sense of quiet and calm begin to permeate your whole being. Visualize a tranquil lake that is a soothing dark sapphire blue. The water is warm to the touch. Around the lake are tall pine trees. On the far side of the lake are two swans swimming. As you sit beside this lake, you feel comfortable and safe.

Focus on a spot on the surface of the lake. As you continue to focus, visualize the face of the deceased person appear on the water's surface. As you take in a deep breath, ask yourself: "What am I feeling?" Are you afraid of death? Are you angry at the person for leaving you? Write down some of your thoughts on your pad. Give yourself time to express your feelings.

Return to your visualization of the lake. Ask yourself: *"What has this loss taught me?"* Take a few minutes to reflect. Are there changes you wish to make sometime in the future? What would you change to make your life more enjoyable? Again, jot down whatever comes to mind.

As you reflect on the loss that has recently occurred, what do the answers to your questions tell you about yourself? Can you be patient with yourself? Can you understand that your loved one didn't leave you?

As you visualize the calm, deep blue lake, become aware that the person you have lost is presenting an opportunity for your growth. Thank your loved one for giving you this opportunity. Thank yourself for opening your mind to this information.

The transition from the physical world to the spiritual world is painless. When a person leaves the physical world, he or she leaves behind a heavy, dense body in a heavy, dense world, which can be compared to removing a winter overcoat. The spirit then enters the more refined energy of the astral world. Nothing is lost except the physical body. The soul and its personality remain intact.

A Letter to Your Loved One

Have a pad, pen, and envelope available. Center your-self with your breathing. When you feel ready, write a letter to the person who has recently passed. Describe your feelings and what you want the deceased person to know. Write what this person meant to you. Write the experiences you shared together that stand out in your mind. Express everything, including any anger, blame, guilt, or whatever you might be repressing. Include how this person has changed your life.

After you have finished your letter, review it to make sure that you have covered everything. Place the letter in the envelope and seal it, and write the name of the person on it. Place the envelope in a safe place.

In a couple of days, you're going to write another letter. This second letter will be a response to your first letter. When you are thoroughly finished with the response, put this letter in another envelope, seal it, and put it with the other. In a few days, take out both letters and read the first letter, then the second. Have your feelings changed? Become aware of what's going on.

Know that your loved ones are only a thought away. You can speak to them, and they can hear you!

*O*ften when a loved one passes, we feel that we have unfinished business with the person. We feel devastated that we may have missed opportunities to share and grow. Understand that we are with family members and friends for many lifetimes, and there will be another life to experience any missed opportunities.

☙ *Forgiveness* ❧

In your relaxed state, visualize yourself sitting in a garden of your own making. Create the environment as you want it. Imagine the various flowers, trees, and plants in your garden. Perhaps there are some benches and a stream or fountain. Off in the distance is a beautiful tree. It may be an oak or a redwood or a fruit tree. There is a mirror hanging from one of its branches.

Walk up to the tree and look into the mirror as closely as possible, until your own reflection can be seen. Observe as much detail as possible in your face. As you see yourself, bring up any expectations that you may have placed on the relationship between your deceased loved one and you. Do you feel guilty about what you did or didn't do? Take the time right now to forgive yourself. You did the best you knew how to do. Say to yourself, "I forgive myself."

Next visualize a pink light of love rising from your heart center. Surround your loved one, any situation between the two of you, and yourself with this pink light of love. See your reflection in the mirror filled with this pink light. Let love fill you up. You realize that it was your loved one's time to go. A soul chooses its time to enter and exit the Earth plane.

Step back from the mirror and look at your garden with a new perspective. The flowers seem brighter. You can hear birds chirping in the trees. You are aware of yourself as a loving, spiritual being. Once you are aware, you cannot hide your light from anyone and anything. You feel very alive and ready to step into your future.

We have to learn to be patient. Things happen in their proper time. There is no use wasting energy worrying about results. Worry and impatience distract us from living in the present and enjoying life as it comes.

∽ Life Changes ∾

Have a pad and pencil by your side. Begin to breathe deeply and relax your whole body. As you sit in the silence, recognize that life is constantly changing. Your body, emotions, life's circumstances, and situations are never static. What happened yesterday is over. Today is a new day, and there will be something different in your life. When you try to control these changes, you get in the way of the divine order of things. Life is about change—this is what makes it so exciting. You are now more mindful of the process of change in your life. You decide to be instrumental in influencing changes for the better in yourself and the world around you. You decide to be proactive and not reactive.

In order to understand fully the impact that change has made in your life, write a list of five major changes that have occurred in your life. As you write, do not judge the experience as good or bad, only as change in your life. Once you have completed your list, one by one write four ways each change has affected you.

1. Has it revealed something in yourself you never knew before?
2. Did it force you to look at life differently?
3. What would you suggest to someone else who is going through a similar experience?
4. The bottom line: Has this change made you a better, stronger, or wiser person?

Review your list of changes. Recognize that each event propelled you in some direction. Maybe your journey had more bumps and curves than you would have liked. However, each change has brought you to where you are right now. If it is not where you want to be, you can take a proactive attitude. Stay positive. When you resist change, you are trying too hard to control the outcome and not paying enough attention to the process.

Enjoy the cosmic dance of life and its changes. You have created your part in it with your thoughts and actions. When making changes, always seek the higher vibrations of love, peace, joy, patience, and abundance.

You are and always will be a spark of the divine. God is not limited, and neither are you. Your home is heaven, and your journey on this Earth is your homework. The key to success on this planet is a keener awareness of your spiritual heritage. When you live every day with spirit in mind, you can never fail.

∽ The Temple of Your Soul ∽

As you become relaxed and centered, imagine that you are high atop a hillside, and below you is a tranquil aquamarine sea. There on the hill is a magnificent, incredible building made of marble and stone. You enter this temple and view the opulence inside. The walls are hand-painted in decorative shades of pastel colors, adorned with massive tapestries picturing gardens and meadows. The floor is designed in an intricate and colorful mosaic tile.

As you walk through this temple, you feel quite pleasant and relaxed in these luxurious surroundings, as if you have been here before. Out of the corner of your eye, you see flashes of tiny elves busy cleaning and repairing the temple. Nothing is amiss; it is perfect in every way. The walls, floors, and ceiling glisten with clarity as if they were sparkling jewels.

As you continue to survey the temple's many grand rooms, you are drawn to the center hall, where a glorious sculpture stands. The form and figure of the model are perfect in every way. You admire it and feel happy just to look at it. Then you realize that it resembles you.

You hear a whisper: *You are in the temple of your soul. You are as magnificent as this temple, perfect and beautiful. Everything you need is available right here.*

A great wave of satisfaction comes over you. You are grateful to be a divine, magnificent creation of God. You feel very good about yourself. You acknowledge your body, which moves through life so that you can perform all your daily activities. You acknowledge your mind for working hard to keep life in order for you and your family. You acknowledge your emotions for letting you feel everything in life. You acknowledge your spirit that gives you life.

As you leave the temple, you look back at this marvelous structure once again. You recognize that your soul is something of loveliness, radiance, and richness. It is a wonderful gift to be treasured and honored always. You are proud of your achievements thus far. You know there are still more to come. From this point on, you make a decision to treat yourself with more love, respect, and kindness.

Some people might feel that they don't deserve happiness or are not worthy of abundance. Others cannot even imagine a life of fullness and joy because they believe it is too good to be true. They think something will go wrong, and for them, it usually does. We are all from the Light and are co-creators with the divine. If we believe in the goodness of the Light that is God, anything is possible.

❦ Tuning In to Abundance ❧

When you are fully relaxed and have opened your psychic centers, visualize yourself in a field under an old oak tree. As you look around, you see beauty everywhere. There is so much beauty in this world that is often overlooked. Nature is perfect, and you are a distinct and unique part of nature.

It is a beautiful, mild day. The sun sends its beautiful rays of gold upon you, and you feel warm and safe. You look to one side and see a big movie screen in the middle of the field. You get up and walk over to it, and click it on. A movie of your life's experiences appears. As you watch, you realize that all those experiences have made you the individual you are today.

Now comes the good part. The movie shows you future events. A myriad of possibilities are presented as your future. The things that you have wanted for a very long time are yours. Perhaps they meet material needs, such as a house, a car, or job. You see a light of gold surrounding all these wonderful gifts and feel quite joyful about what is to come. You decide to have more faith in the goodness that life has to offer. You open your arms and receive this good into your heart. Feel that good will expanding your heart chakra. Say to yourself, *"I am willing to receive all the good that life has in store for me."* Perhaps you see yourself in the future with a houseful of friends having a big party. You might see yourself involved in the artistic endeavors you have always dreamed about. Right there on the screen is a world that you always wanted to live in. You have enough money so financial worries are a thing of the past. You no longer tie your belief into the economic beliefs of the times. There is enough for everyone, and that includes you. This new knowledge gives you a true sense of financial freedom. See yourself living your dream and enjoying abundance. There is great joy in having what you want.

As you watch your future life, you know that right now you are raising your consciousness to bring about what you see on the screen. There is no time in spirit. The present and the future are happening simultaneously. All that negativity you have been feeling is turning positive. All the fear you have been harboring inside is disintegrating into nothing. Love is filling you and replacing the fear. When you come from a place of love, anything is possible. The only thing keeping you from what you want is your belief that it is not possible. Believe in the love because love will create what you want. Fear keeps your dreams from coming true.

At this very moment, a door appears on the screen. It says ABUNDANCE. You see yourself opening this door and walking through. All the riches of the universe are waiting for you. You see it for yourself and believe you can have these wonderful treasures. You feel so fulfilled and happy watching all this on the screen. You are finished for now, but you can always return to watch again.

You walk back to the tree and sit down under it.

All the positive feelings are inside you. Each day you live your dreams because you are creating them with love in your heart. Slowly you become aware of yourself back in your room. Open your arms and say, *"I receive my riches every day."*

You have an important contribution to make on this Earth. Do not waste precious time in negative emotions and fear. Look at life with the knowledge that what you do affects everyone. Consider your thoughts and actions wisely.

✑ Your Book of Life ✑

As you tune in to the quiet inside, become aware of the space two feet in front of your third eye center. As you concentrate of this spot, visualize a golden point of light. Focus your awareness on this spot of light. As you focus on it, the spot grows larger. Look into the center of this light and notice that its bright golden rays expand to fill the room. Keep your focus on the light until you begin to feel enveloped in the light and become the light.

Relax and enjoy this sensation of being in the light and then start moving through the light into a tunnel. On the other side of the tunnel is your spirit guide waiting for you. You follow your guide, and he or she leads you to a golden palace. It is the Institution of

Understanding. You enter this beautiful structure with your guide and are led down a great hall. Your guide points to a door, and it opens automatically. You enter a large room. In the center of the room is a long table made of gold. Seated around the table are other radiant beings. These are all your spirit guides. Their expressions are of love and compassion, and you can feel this energy radiating from them.

As your guides begin to communicate telepathically, they show you a large golden chair to sit in. Once again you feel their love. One by one, each guide communicates how he or she helps you on Earth. When you get to your master guide, he or she hands you a book bound in leather. The title is imprinted in gold leaf: *My Book of Life*. You open the book and begin to look through its pages. The first page illustrates your birth. Take your time and go through the pages slowly. You begin to have a better understanding of the various events in your life. Perhaps you see a word, a picture, or a face. At the bottom of the page is a note. It is the lesson you have learned from that experience. You realize that there are no good or bad experiences— only experiences that have helped your soul to grow.

You reach the middle of the book. The page depicts your life as it is right now. You look at the bottom of the page and notice it is blank. What is the lesson you are learning at this time? The rest of the book is blank. Your guides smile at you with compassion in their eyes. One of them hands you a pen and asks you to write what you are willing to change for the future. There is no judgment. On the blank page you write a word or a sentence. This is what you are ready to do to move forward in your life.

When you are finished, your guides indicate a space on one of the bookshelves in the room. You place your book there, and notice many books on the shelf. They are books about other lifetimes you have had. All the records of all your lifetimes are on these shelves.

You hug your guides and thank them for their love and direction. They smile with thoughts of encouragement. *You are never alone,* they say. *We will always be around to assist you.* You leave the building filled with courage and optimism about the rest of your life. With gratitude and appreciation for all that you have been given, you look forward to what spirit has in store for you.

Each person incarnates on Earth at a different level of growth. Each one needs to go through different experiences to gain wisdom and expand his or her awareness of life. When we open our minds and hearts to the higher aspects of life, we can use our elevated awareness to inspire and help others.

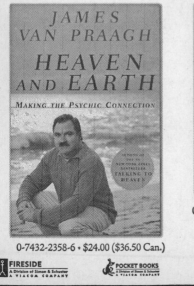
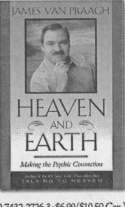